SURFSEA'S DAY AT THE BEACH

MYRA MIDDLE

To order additional copies of this book, contact:
Xlibris
844-714-8691
www.Xlibris.com
Orders@Xlibris.com

ISBN: Softcover   978-1-6698-5861-4
       EBook   978-1-6698-5862-1

Print information available on the last page

Rev. date: 05/18/2023

SURFSEA'S DAY AT THE BEACH

It is July 1st, and it is Surfsea's 10th birthday. It is a beautiful day with a bright blue sky, lots of sunshine, and a warm gentle breeze. Surfsea's parents have promised him a day at the beach on his birthday, and it looks like he will get his wish today. Surfsea loves the beach, and he especially loves to go surfing. His mom, Seamo, decides that they will celebrate his birthday with a family picnic on the beach. His mom starts preparing their picnic lunch. Since today is Surfsea's birthday, he will be treated to his favorite food of canned sardines. He is allowed to eat one whole can by himself, but his mom will pack enough for everyone. He will also have a delicious seaweed birthday cake and clam juice, also his favourites. On a regular day, his family eats mostly herring; but today is party time, and Surfsea is excited and cannot wait to go. He grabs his swim trunks, life jacket, swim goggles, sun hat, sunglasses and sunscreen and puts them in his beach bag. Surfing is his favorite sport. In fact, his mom was a surfer when she was younger, and that's how he got his name. From the time he was little, he could not wait to go to the beach and watch the surfers ride the waves. Everyone was always smiling and laughing when they were surfing. Until today, Surfsea rode only on children's surfboards near the shore. Now he has a new surfboard, a birthday gift from his parents, and this is the day he will use it for the first time. He cannot wait to jump on it and ride the big waves himself. Seamo tells everyone to get ready for the beach. Seada picks up the picnic basket, Seamo takes the beach towels, and the kids all grab their beach bags and head to the beach. On this beautiful day, there should be lots of waves rolling onto shore. Better still, the water is clear, warm, and perfect for surfing.

After arriving at the beach, the whole family searches for a spot where the sand is nice and dry, and where there are no rough stones in the water that could cut their feet.

The beach is very crowded, but Seada finds a great spot. Everyone starts laying their towels on the sand and changing into their swimwear. They all plan to go swimming and have fun in the water under the beautiful hot sun. They put on sunscreen, swimwear, life jackets, sunglasses, and hats. Since Surfsea will be surfing, he does not wear his hat, and he chooses to wear his goggles instead of his sunglasses. He is all ready to hit the waves.

Surfsea grabs his surfboard and heads to the ocean. He paddles out to catch a wave. Suddenly, he sees a big wave and gets in position on his surfboard to ride it back to shore. On his first attempt, he has a short, but thrilling ride before he falls off. It takes Surfsea a few more rides to get used to his new, longer board. He continued riding the waves over and over until his legs got very tired.

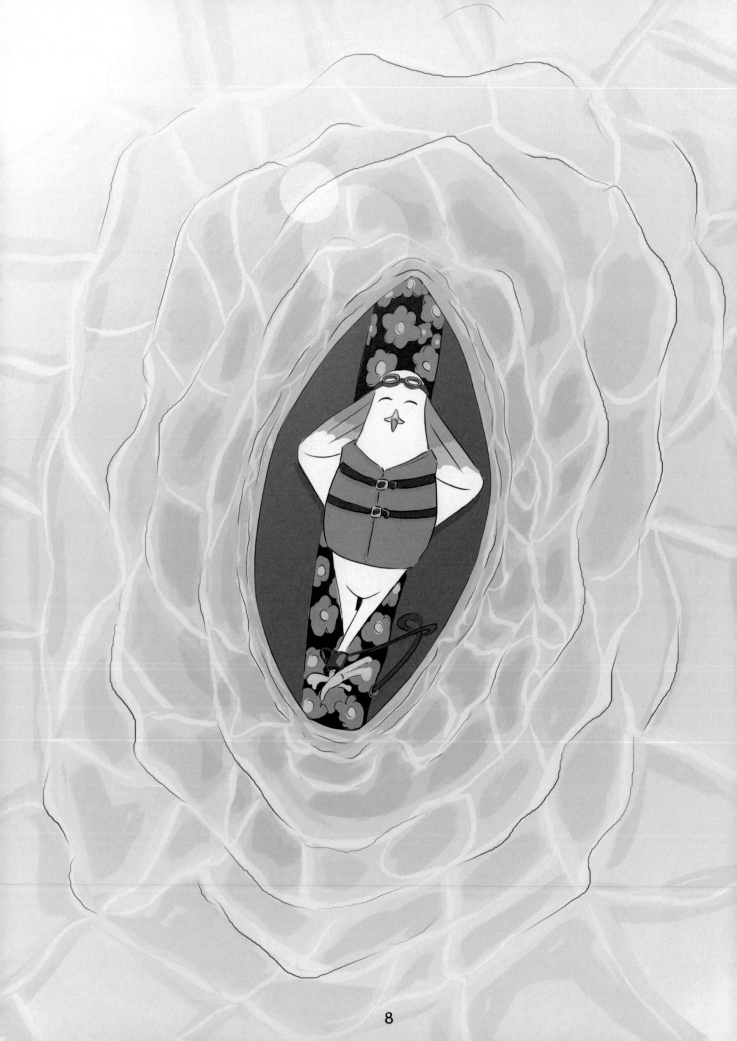

At that point, he lies down on his surfboard and decides to rest for a while. He looks around admiring the beautiful scenery of the shoreline and all the people enjoying this day, just like he is. While he is still resting, he notices that many people are getting out of the water and heading for the beach. Some look like they are in a hurry. Surfsea does not know what all the commotion is about, but he is going to find out for himself.

When he turns his head around and looks out to sea, he sees a big fin sticking out of the water. And, it is coming towards him! It is a shark, he thought! Now he knows why everyone is rushing to the shore and decides he will do the same. He turns his surfboard directly towards the beach and starts paddling frantically. The shark is catching up to him, and he figures he is doomed! He thinks he is about to become a snack for a big shark. This is not going to be a very good birthday after all! Surfsea decides he cannot outswim the shark, so he lies down on his board and does not move. He is even afraid to blink his eyes. He keeps them closed and waits for the worse. He feels the shark swim by him when his surfboard moves, but nothing happens. He is still alive! He opens his eyes and sees the shark swimming towards the shore, and it is now in shallow water and almost on the beach. On a closer look, Surfsea realizes it is not a shark after all. Instead, it is an orca or killer whale, which is the type of whale he saw at Sea World doing tricks in the water. He saw them jumping, bouncing balls on their snouts, and splashing water on the spectators with their tails and their mouths. Surfsea wonders why this orca is heading to the beach, which does not seem right. He follows the whale to the beach, and there he discovers the whale is struggling to breathe.

At that point, Surfsea jumps on the whale's head to have a look at its blowhole, through which the whale breathes. It appears something is stuck in there, and that is why the whale cannot breathe. Surfsea has to help this whale, or else it will die. He sticks his beak down the whale's blowhole and starts pulling on some object that is lodged there. He pulls and pulls, but he cannot pull it out. He yells for help. "Please someone come and help me save this whale. It cannot breathe." After hearing his cry for help, his brother, Sportsea, and Seada come to the rescue. All three stand on the whale's head with their beaks inside its blowhole trying to remove the object. Finally, they get a good grip on it and begin pulling it out.

When the object is removed, they discover it is a large clear plastic garbage bag. Everyone on the beach is applauding. Surfsea, his dad, and his brother have saved the whale's life.

Now, they need to get the whale back into the water so it can swim out to sea. People see what they are trying to do and several come to help. Some begin throwing water on the whale with their kids' sand buckets to keep it wet, while others are tugging at it with ropes to drag it back out to sea. Finally, the whale is free. Before the whale swims too far away, it breeches out of the water and waves its tail as if to say thank you and goodbye.

Surfsea suddenly is very hungry, and his mom decides it is time for their family picnic. She spreads her picnic blanket on the sand, and the whole family gathers around to share the food. Surfsea eats a whole can of sardines himself, and his mom serves him the first piece of his birthday cake, along with some clam juice. While they are eating, the family praises Surfsea for spotting the whale and saving its life. His father says, "Surfsea, you did a wonderful thing today on your tenth birthday. You spotted a whale in trouble, and you saved its life. That is an amazing thing, and one that you will never forget." Surfsea thanks his dad and Sportsea for their help, and asks his dad how the whale got a garbage bag caught in its blowhole in the first place. His father says, "Well son, some people don't think about the animals who live in the oceans, and they dump their garbage there, including plastic bags, bottles, straws, and many other things. Our oceans are polluted with all kinds of garbage, and the sea animals are dying because of it. We have to do something about it for the future of our oceans and our sea animals. We need to educate people about the dangers of throwing things in the ocean that can injure or even kill the sea animals. That whale is lucky! You spotted that it was in trouble and you took action to help it. Because of you, it is still alive. Some dolphins, whales, tuna, sharks, turtles, and other sea animals are not so lucky. Many of them die every year when they become tangled in nylon fishing lines, nets, and when they eat plastic bottles, straws, and now, face masks, that people have dumped in the oceans. Surfsea, I think this is your best birthday gift ever! I am so proud of you for what you did today. You taught us all an important lesson."

Seamo picks up the clear plastic bag that was removed from the whale's blowhole and thinks of ways she can use it. She decides it will make a perfect canopy for her children's tree house. She is always making new things from discarded objects. As the sun starts to set, Seamo tells her family to pack up their belongings and head back home. It was a very eventful tenth birthday for Surfsea after all. He is exhausted, but he is very happy! As soon as he gets home, he lies down on his special feather pillow and falls asleep.

AN EAST COAST SEAGULL FAMILY
By Myra Middle

Grandparents
Seapa—Grandfather seagull—Seamo's Father
Seama—Grandmother seagull—Seamo's Mother

Parents
Seada—Father seagull+
Seamo—Mother seagull

The rest of the family is as follows:

Males
Sportsea—Oldest male
Surfsea—Second oldest male
Sooksea—Youngest male

Females
Swimsea—Oldest female
Skillsea—Second oldest female
Sweetsea—Youngest female and the baby

Michael Mito

Since this story involves an encounter with a whale, I'm dedicating this book to my older son, Michael, whose father was involved with the whaling industry in Newfoundland and Iceland in the early 1970s. Michael was only one year old when he saw a whale for the first time at the whaling station in Iceland. Whaling was banned in Newfoundland in 1972. There was much controversy over the killing of whales, and pressure was put on countries to ban it around the world forever. Most countries were in favour, but a few are still whaling to this day.

Emi Elan

I'm also dedicating this book to my younger grand-daughter, Emi Elan, who is fascinated with almost everything she sees. She is curious, like all children, but also very intuitive. She loves to take on tasks well beyond her years, and she will figure things out for herself. Both Emi and her sister Mila, to whom I dedicated Rabi's Hallowe'en Adventure, love the stories I tell them like this one, usually at bedtime. Sometimes they enjoy making up their own stories to tell me and have become very imaginative and creative storytellers themselves.

Each of my books has a lesson, which in this particular book is about pollution in our oceans, especially items such as plastic bottles, bags, fishing line, straws, nets, and many other things. Filling our oceans with trash has got to stop. We have to start educating people about the effects this type of trash has on our sea animals. Many die every year when they encounter them in the ocean, their home.

The Pictures of the Sea Animals presented here show their encounters with plastics and other trash found in the oceans. *Source: The Internet: Sea Animals Caught in Plastics.*

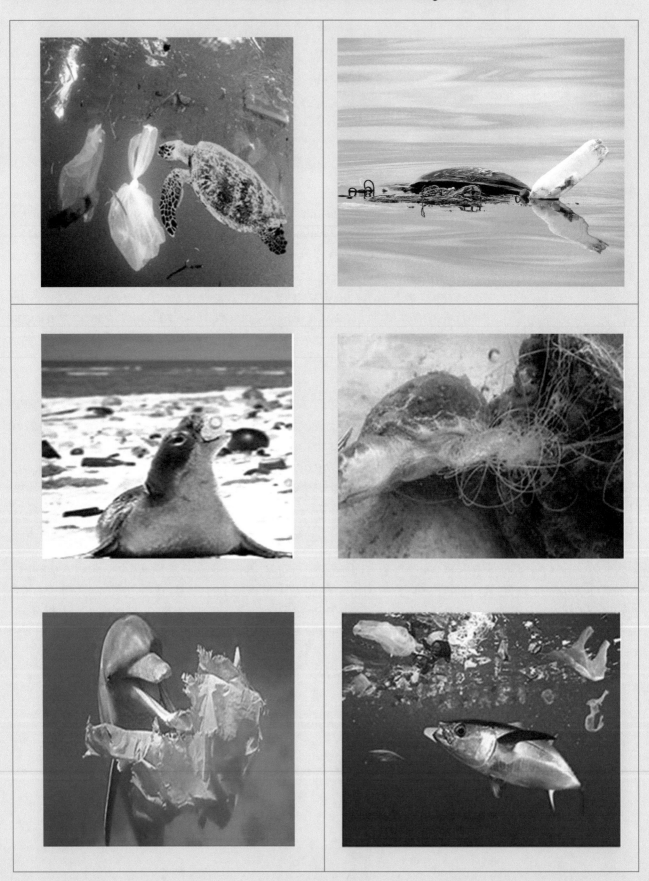

These pictures are placed in this book to reinforce the lesson about the amount of plastics and other trash that is found in our oceans and how it affects the lives of the sea animals when they eat it or get entangled in it. They are unable to escape on their own and will most likely die as a result. It is terrible, and it is getting worse every year. It is time we all show respect for our environment and for the land and sea animals who share this planet with us. Let's start by cleaning up our oceans.

Killer whales or Orcas are the largest of the dolphin family of whales. They are intelligent animals and can be taught to do tricks in the water. These are the type of whales that we see at Sea World and Marineland performing their skills, such as swimming on their tails, bouncing balls on their snouts, and splashing water with their tails and mouths on the spectators. They are rewarded with small fish after they perform.

Source: The Internet

An East Coast Seagull is a common sight around the beaches of the Atlantic Ocean. Seagulls are also around shopping malls searching for scrap food. An interesting fact about seagulls is they make good parents and both take care of their young by feeding and protecting them. They are also very smart and good hunters for food. They can drink both salt and fresh water.

Source: The Internet

An Atlantic coast beach where people can go surfing

Source: The Internet